STATIONERY McKENZIE'S

Submitted by Richard & Robin Pompeo

Reflections

Quincy & the South Shore

A pictorial history

Volume 1

Published by

The Patriot Ledger

James F. Plugh, Publisher

Printed in the U.S.A. by Quebecor World, Kingsport, Tennessee

ISBN 0-9745485-0-2

ON THE COVER
Nine-year-old Arthur "Bud" Bennette of Quincy finds peace of mind on Town River Bay.
Submitted by Jim Bennette

ACKNOWLEDGEMENTS

Reflections
Quincy & the South Shore

THE PATRIOT LEDGER PROJECT STAFF:

Elayne V. Quinn, Project Director
Lisa Barstow, Research and Writing
Kristine Lewis, Project Coordinator
Kevin Oberbeck, Book Production and Design
Mark Seel, Copywriter
Peter Ricardi and Richard Carrus, Photo Scanners

SPECIAL THANKS TO:

Alden House Museum
Brookdale River Bay Club
Cohasset Historical Society
Edward Feldman
Connie Gibbs
Paul Kelsch
Lydia Drake Branch Library
North Scituate Library
The Patriot Ledger Library
Plymouth Library Association
Kerri Resmini
Mary Clark, Thomas Crane Library
Thomas M. Galvin, the Thomas M. Galvin Collection
Tufts Library Inc.
Ron Welby

We'd also like to express our deep appreciation to all who shared their photos and their stories for **Reflections: Quincy and the South Shore**. Special effort was made to ensure the accuracy of information accompanying these photographs. However, information written on the backs of photographs, dates and events recalled by individuals may not have been exact, so this book should not be relied upon for historical accuracy. We welcome corrected and additional information, which will be forwarded to the appropriate individual, archives or museum. Please forward information in writing to: *The Patriot Ledger*, Communications Department, P.O. Box 699159, Quincy, MA 02269-9159.

PREFACE

"We are tied to the ocean. And when we go back to the sea—whether it is to sail or to watch it—we are going back from whence we came."
— John F. Kennedy

Few quotations could better capture the essence of **Reflections: Quincy and the South Shore** and the purpose and soul of this project. Boating, fishing, sailing, swimming, shipbuilding, all hold such a fundamental place in the history of Quincy and the South Shore. Perhaps more than any other element, the water around us floods our lives with memories and perspective.

Reflections: Quincy and the South Shore is a different type of look at ourselves. It is a look from within at the people, places, and passions of our lives—offered in reverence by the subjects themselves and those who are committed to their legacy.

Over a period of months, *The Patriot Ledger* gathered from readers their life stories told by their own family photographs taken before 1960. People at work in the quarries. People at play on Nantasket Beach. People at home: cooking, laughing, loving. Some images are humorous and irreverent. Others show intense courage and commitment. Still more convey the grit and tenacity demonstrated by ordinary people who have built this extraordinary region we call the South Shore with their own hearts and hands.

As you peruse these pages, we at *The Patriot Ledger* believe you will immediately recognize not only the historical value of this unique project, but also the granite on which our collective lives in Quincy and the South Shore are laid.

Sincerely,

James F. Plugh, Publisher, *The Patriot Ledger*

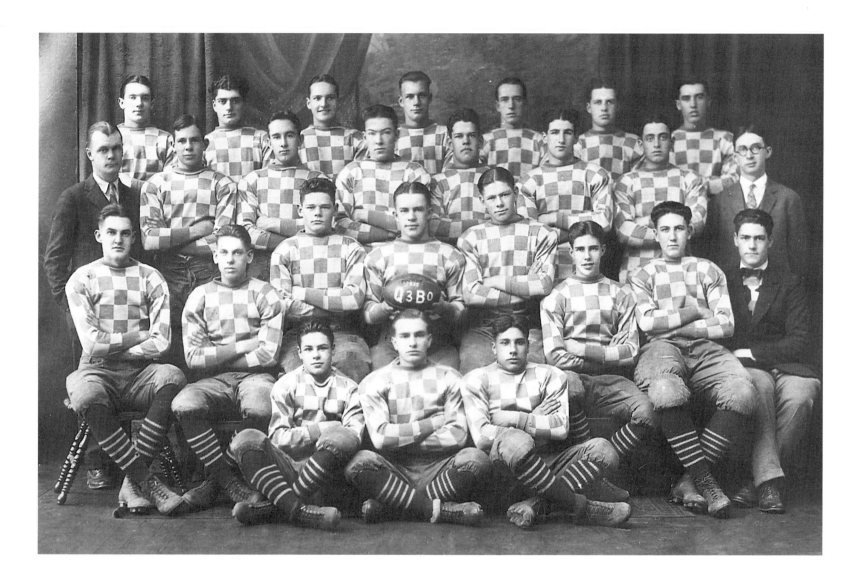

QUINCY HIGH SCHOOL FOOTBALL 1925

Munrow MacLean (second row, third from right) and Jim LeCain (second row, second from left) played football for
Quincy High while in school. Years later, Monrow returned to Quincy High and became the team's head coach.
Submitted by Jean Ann Phinney

UP ON THE ROOFTOP

During breaks at Quincy City Hospital, these four nurses including Helen Crowell, Marie Martinelli and Mary McNaughton Peck often went up to their rooftop "patio" to enjoy a little conversation and the view.
Submitted by Marie (Martinelli) Fehlow

SUNDAY BEST

Shirley (Johnson) Back, age 17, stands in Quincy Square on her way to church.
Submitted by Shirley Back

FIRST LADY

Florence Joyce was the first woman ever interviewed and hired to be a welder at the Fore River Shipyard. Florence was fascinated with welding and loved being part of the war effort. She quickly moved through her training and was grateful for the acceptance she and her female colleagues received from their male counterparts.

Submitted by Florence Joyce

TRICK OR TREAT

Peter Pan (a.k.a. Lyda Killory), bottom left, who performed on the Vaudeville stage, loved to entertain friends and spooks alike, as she did during this 1946 Halloween Party at her Sachem Street, Wollaston home. Accompanied by her ukulele, "Ain't She Sweet" was Lyda's favorite number–making the friends who survived the scary skeletons and other decorative frights wonder whether she's more salty than sweet!

Submitted by Judy Spiegel

MAN OF MANY INTERESTS

William J. Cunniff of Quincy worked at the Fore River Shipyard (Local 188) as a pipefitter and later became an engineer on a yacht. A left-handed pitcher, he briefly played pro baseball until his yacht boss wouldn't allow him to do both—he opted for more predictable income. Cunniff eventually became Business Manager of Pipefitters Local 537 and was co-owner with Bill Ballon of a refrigeration and air conditioning school in Quincy. Cunniff married Delma Brunet, also of Quincy. He is seen here with the car in which he journeyed 10,000 miles across America.
Submitted by Laurie Strout

MEMORIES OF HOME

Ethel (Evanson) Taylor grew up on White Street in South Weymouth. Twenty-five years after moving from her family home and starting a family of her own, she was referred to a particular seamstress to tailor her son's Navy uniform. That seamstress now lived in the house that was Ethel's childhood family home.
Submitted by Wendy Taylor

MUSCLE CAR

Val Perry and his son Bob knew cars. This customized "Ford by Muggsy" (of
Muggsy's Tire Shop) drew almost as much attention in 1927 as the good lookers
inside! Bob Perry owned a Shell Station on Sea Street in Quincy, and their
"love of autos legacy" is a third generation who have become mechanics.
Submitted by Lorrayne Paolucci

YOU GO GIRL!

Good thing for Paul Tobin that his wife Ethel (Bishop) was as nervy as she was cute!
Ethel's adventurous spirit provided a good match for Paul's riskier interests. Ethel and
Paul took long rides on his Indian motorcycle. And since Paul was a pilot, Ethel also
went on many flights. After the kids came along, things settled down a bit but she
continued to work from home as a hairdresser. The Tobins made their home in Quincy.
Submitted by Paul Tobin

GEARING UP FOR WORK

Management, professional workers and laborers from Boston Gear gather together for a company photo in front of the Hayward Street facility, in the area of North Quincy known as Norfolk Downs. The photo was taken not long after the company's move from Charlestown in 1906. The early work force at the company was dominated by male, European immigrants, until World War II brought a large number of women into the workplace. After the war, many blue-collar women were moved into office jobs.

Submitted by John Croto, Boston Gear

BUILDING GENERATIONS

Ephraim and Mary Kilcup with daughter Edith (center) lived at 275 Manet Avenue in Houghs Neck, adjacent to E.J.'s business. To the left of the home was the local fire house. A devastating blaze took the Kilcup's home and business, as well as young Edith's new velvet Christmas dress. But it didn't take away their spirit. E.J. rebuilt the home, and two more Kilcup generations lived there (the Rowes and the Ryders). The house remains today. In the background (left) is the Atherton Hough School. This photo was taken in 1910.

Submitted by Edith Ryder

CIVIL SERVANT

Jeremiah Dennison served in the Civil War and later opened the J. Dennison general store on School Street in Stoughton.
He and his wife Bridget had three daughters Catherine, Mary and Alice. Jeremiah died at age 45.
Submitted by Margaret Sweeney

FIVE AND DIME TIMES

The Adams Building in downtown Quincy was the home of the city's first F.W. Woolworth & Co. Store. Manager George B. Monroe (last doorway on right) and Bookkeeper Annie Nightingale (middle doorway, first on left) are seen under the gas lamps with fellow 1912 employees. The photo is understood to have been taken by Quincy photographer A.W. Pierce, whose studio was above the store.
Submitted by John Lukkanen

SISTER SISTER

Blithe-spirited smiles and games mark this sisterhood. Sisters Hilja and Aili Maki frolic on their family's Braintree farmland in 1927 on the terrain where South Shore Plaza now stands. Rhythmic hand clapping and gesturing games remain a popular pastime for schoolgirls and sisters today.
Submitted by Cathy Heath

FAMOUS FRIEND

A famous friend of the Pallotta family of Scituate was former Boston Mayor and Massachusetts Governor Maurice Tobin, seen here as a guest at the Pallotta family's cottage at Peggotty Beach. In his suit and tie, the Governor must have felt quite warm amidst the lovely Pallotta ladies in their summer wear. Three years after this photo, in 1948, former Gov. Tobin was appointed United States Secretary of Labor under President Harry S. Truman. Tobin's sudden death in 1953 brought the former President to Holy Cross Cathedral to mourn. In 1967, the well-known toll-bridge connecting Boston to the North was renamed for the former statesman.
Submitted by Lorraine (Pallotta) Quinn

GARDEN VARIETY FUN

As grandpa Robert Grant chopped down a tree to make
way for a garden, grandchildren Robert Iacobucci and
Kathleen Iacobucci Kerr frolicked on the downed limbs.
Submitted by Kathleen Kerr

LOUNGING AROUND

Arthur "Sunny" Pallotta of Medford and his friend Michael Vassalotti
of Newton lounge around on the porch of the Pallotta family cottage at
Peggotty Beach in Scituate.
Submitted by Lorraine Quinn

END OF AN ERA

Dorothy Maranda Kelly like many South Shore women, were active in the United Service Organization (USO) and supporting the war effort. This gathering in August of 1946, which included billiards, shuffle board, refreshments, drinking and dancing, marked the close of Quincy's USO.
Submitted by Dorothy Kelly

THE GRADUATE

On her graduation day from Weymouth High School in 1947, Ethel (Evanson) Taylor came to Fogg Library to have her picture taken. Taking special occasion photographs on the steps of the library was a popular way to memorialize important events.
Submitted by Wendy Taylor

SUFFRAGETTE CITY

Frank Burgess, president of Boston Gear Works, was not only a central business leader in Quincy, he and his wife Lizzy were actively involved in political and social causes. Amidst a parochial civic and work force environment, Burgess was a strong supporter of the Suffragette movement. Boston Gear Works also advanced a host of internal policies that integrated blue and white collar workers and set progressive standards to provide housing, education and financial security for their employees.

Submitted by John Croto, Boston Gear

PICTURE THAT

Alves Photo Finishing served the community for 75 years before it closed in 2001. In 1969, it was entered into the Photo Marketing Association Hall of Fame.
Submitted by Joan Greifeld

IRON MEN

Metal parts shake, rattle and hum for the engineers and laborers at Boston Gear. Boston "gears" were used in World War II torpedoes.
Submitted by Dan Murphy, Boston Gear

NOW THOSE ARE WHITE WALLS!

Val "Muggzy" Perry moved his Cambridge tire store to Quincy Point shortly before this 1927 photo of the Washington Street shop was taken. The "Smiling Maestro", as he was known to customers and neighbors, shared space with Johnny's Battery Service Station.
Submitted by Lorrayne Paolucci

THE CHECK'S IN THE MAIL

Benjamin Lawson Smith was born in Charlotte, NC, and eventually moved to Quincy to assume the position of Bookkeeper at the Fore River Shipyard. Nearly a hundred years before business casual came into fashion, Mr. Smith is seen here at the shipyard's business office with his ledger book and other tools of the trade.
Submitted by Phil Smith

Submitted by Ann Ramponi

Submitted by Dave Becker

Submitted by Gwen Senger

Submitted by Catherine Heath

Submitted by Mary Quinn

Submitted by Charles & Eileen Loring

Submitted by Stephen Haskel

Submitted by Lorraine Quinn

Submitted by Gayle Sheehan

Submitted by Joseph Walsh

READDY TO GET INVOLVED

The Readdys of Quincy were active and involved people, who also knew the value of relaxation – like here on the waters of Hingham. Vincent Readdy was active in the Sacred Heart Parish and the Knights of Columbus. He also served as a trustee of the Thomas Crane Library. Margaret (Lipp) Readdy was active in the Red Cross and the PTA of the Montclair School. Both lived in Quincy for over 60 years.
Submitted by Marjorie Sullivan

OUTING

A little poker, a little smoke, and lots of food! The Maligno family, (left to right) brothers Charles and Michael with sister Millie Ciapetti take part in a National Guard outing at Faxon Park. Charles "Mitty" worked at the Fore River Shipyard and Michael for Boston Gear Works. Millie worked at the Penn Street housecoat factory in Quincy.
Submitted by Fran Fruzzetti

CALLING ALL SPORTS

All-around sportsman Wilfred LeVangie (pictured with pipe) loved to hunt near his family farm at Braintree Five Corners – where the family home remains. During the 1920s, Wilfred also played baseball in Weymouth on the team that is now known as the Cranberry League's Braintree White Sox.
Submitted by Anne O'Donnell

FRESH FISH

Nothing tastes as good as your own daily catch. Elmer Norling got his in Plymouth.
Submitted by Merrilee Swan

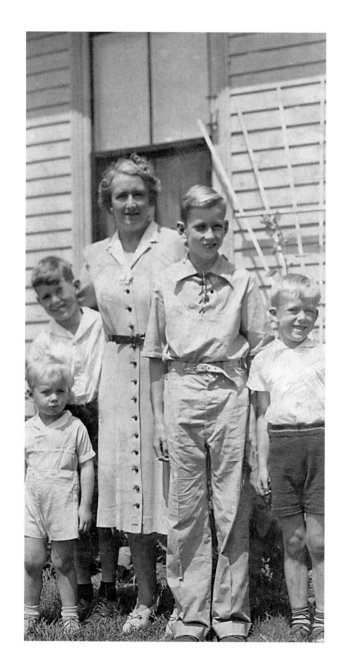

THE SMITH FAMILY

In 1905, Benjamin Lawson Smith and his wife Agnes posed in front of their home with their children Benjamin Jr., Robert, Ernie and Katherine. Although born in North Carolina, Mr. Smith eventually moved to Quincy and worked as a bookkeeper at The Fore River Shipyard. Later in his career he was employed at *The Patriot Ledger*.
Submitted by Phil Smith

BROTHERLY LOVE

Tom Masterson, bottom left, with older brothers John, Jim, Paul and mother Frances in 1941 at their home on Clay Street in Quincy. The home is still there today, and the brothers continue to get together monthly for dinner.
Submitted by Tom Masterson

CLASSIC REUNION

Students from the Noah Torrey School in South Braintree wave America's 48-star flag during a 1915 class photograph.
Years later, some students returned to take advantage of senior care services offered in the building.
Submitted by Anne O'Donnell

FAMILY FORD

Jannell Motor Co. is one of the oldest family-run Ford dealerships in America. This photo, taken in the early 1930s, shows the dealership at its original location in Weymouth. In 1993, the dealership moved to Hanover, but the business still maintains an auto body and car rental facility in Weymouth.

Submitted by Ned and Joe Jannell

RUNNING ON EMPTY

Business must have been slow at this Shell Station on Washington Street in Weymouth. Otherwise, attendant Frank Grant may have unknowingly spurred on the self-service movement!

Submitted by David Belcher

CLEAN MACHINE

Imagine the lucky girls that got invited to cruise the Point in this gleaming '52 Chevy! Aare Valja and brothers John and Tom Murray (left to right) spruce it up so they'll all be looking good for the weekend. Tom was affectionately known by friends as the "Mayor of Quincy Point." After his death, a plaque was erected in 1994 at Avalon Beach remembering Tom as a "friend to the neighborhood."
Submitted by Jean Liben

DAD'S PRIDE

Edward W. Norling of Braintree was just so cute his dad couldn't help but capture it!
Submitted by Merrilee Swan

CLASSIC PHOTO

Florence Nightingale (far right) bore quite a famous name!
She is pictured here with her classmates at the John Hancock
School, Quincy in 1909.
Submitted by John Laukkanen

TYPE "A" MOM

Sophia LeVangie of Braintree was always busy
doing something! As if raising 12 children didn't
keep her busy enough, Sophia always had her black
bag with her, toting her latest needlework project.
Submitted by Anne O'Donnell

WOMEN OF HONOR

The Women's Guild of Christ Church Episcopal in Quincy is known to be Quincy's oldest women's club. Seen here
celebrating their 50th anniversary, the guild would raise money that supported various ministries of the church,
including overseas missionary efforts. The guild is still active and meeting regularly today.
Submitted by David Barton

SWEET CHILD OF MINE

Two-year old Loretta Coletti with father, Val, in front of their home on Doble Street in West Quincy in 1942. Val owned a local machine shop and garage for many years.
Submitted by Ann Ramponi

EARLY TRAINING

Gene Coletti and son Richard visiting Edaville Railroad in Carver. Virginia Coletti, Gene's wife, took this photo, but the family photographer was Gene, who has volumes of images chronicling the events and happenings of their large extended family. Gene was a machinist for 42 years at Boston Gear Works. Richard has two children of his own that he, too, has brought to Edaville.
Submitted by Ann Ramponi

WOLLASTON YACHT CLUB

This family photo of Laurie (Cunniff) Strout shows the Wollaston Yacht Club before it was destroyed by winter ice in the late 1950s. The Yacht Club was later rebuilt and remains today at the same location.
Submitted by Laurie Strout

CRIME REPORTER

Catherine Schofield Delargy was a woman ahead of her time. Seen here in the late 1920s driving in front of the Jackson Square Tavern with her traveling companion Rex, Catherine was a police reporter for the *Boston Record American* newspaper covering Quincy and the South Shore. Her husband, Bill Delargy, was a police beat photographer for the *Record American* assigned to Quincy. Catherine's sister, Barbara Allen, was that paper's society reporter.
Submitted by Susan Jeffrey

HAZARDOUS WORK

With Quincy's rich stores of granite, stone-cutting for grave markers was an important industry – but it was not without its hazards. Many stone masons died prematurely of tuberculosis from inhaling stone dust, an unknown risk. Mitchell Favaeau (third from left) is seen with fellow masons in 1911. *Submitted by Eleanor Graff*

FINNISH WORK

Quincy's quarries provided jobs for many European immigrants. Records indicate that the first Finns in Quincy settled in the year 1886 and included Tuomas Hakala, who worked as a quarryman for the Granite Railway Company. These Finnish quarrymen were employed at Greyrock Quarry during the 1920s: Messrs. Hakoniemi, Luoma, Myylimaki (top, left to right), Hirvimaki (lower left in overalls) and Sevela (lower left in white shirt). *Submitted by Doug Luoma*

FLYING OFF FALLON

Generations of dare devils dove from atop Quincy's famous quarries. This group at Fallon's
Quarry was photographed by Quincy native Gene Coletti during the mid 1940s.
Submitted by Ann Ramponi

FINE FAMILY

Ernest Sturgis bought his home at 6 Pearl Street in Weymouth for $2,000 in 1940. His wife Eileen kept busy as a wife, mother, and talented seamstress who made elegant clothes for her girls. Daughters Elizabeth, Joan, and Joyce fashion their togs in front of the 1951 Chevy. Ernest and Eileen still live in the house on Pearl Street.
Submitted by Ernest Sturgis

SWEET MEMORIES

Peter Joyce Jr. joins Aunt Kay (Kathryn Looby), and cousins Janet, Jerry and Paul Looby in their Middle Street, Weymouth kitchen for cupcakes on Easter. Kay would have been a familiar face to many patrons of both Lumbs Restaurant and the Red Coach Grill in Braintree, where she worked as a waitress for many years.
Submitted by Paula Ivanoskos

OUR GANG

The peach schnapps pours freely at this Christmas celebration reuniting the boy-
hood friends after their return from the service. Quincy natives all, (seated front left
to right) Sam Garlisi, Russ Corsini, Jimmy Corbett, Larry Mullane, (standing rear)
John Mullane and Joe Luiso ring in the holiday at the Luiso home. Sam Garlisi
owned Riverside Auto Body in Braintree for more than 20 years and was a former
commissioner and initial developer of Pond Meadow Park in Braintree/Weymouth.
Submitted by Melissa Garlisi

PRINCIPAL DUTY

Leo Madden, principal, takes a group of Bicknell
Junior High students to the new Johnson School
in Weymouth – named after Eldon Johnson,
a soldier killed in action in World War II.
Submitted by Ernest Sturgis

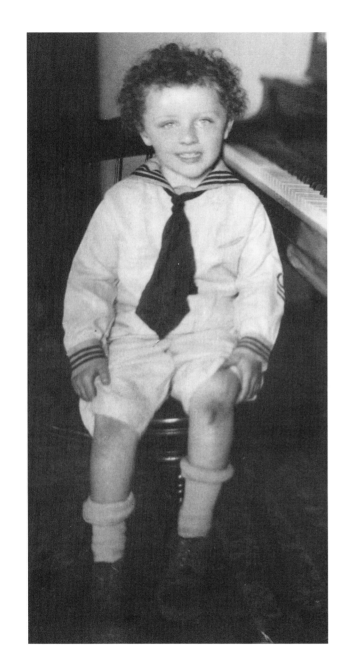

SON OF THE SEA

Young Robert Rudolf's artistic passion would turn from music to painting as the little sailor man grew to become a seascape painter, when he wasn't at work as a rigger at the Fore River Shipyard. His love of the sea was nurtured early on by father Charles who was a rigger at Quincy Adams Yacht Yard adjacent to their home on Palmer Street. Robert would live all his years in his native Quincy. He had eight children.
Submitted by Robin Ravita

COHASSET WATERS

Dorothy Montgomery, here in 1940, summered in Cohasset and loved rowing on the harbor. Captain John Smith is said to have landed in Cohasset Harbor in 1614.
Submitted by Carol Archer

THE YACHTSMAN

Charles Rudolf worked in the early to mid-1900s at the Quincy Adams Yacht Yard on Palmer Street as a rigger and lived in a house next door.
Seen here tending to the bow line, Rudolf passed his love of the water on to son Robert, who would become a rigger for the Fore River Shipyard.
Submitted by Robin Ravida

LOGGING ON

Cousins Mary Jane Kenney, Joseph Messier and Richard Loud play with an old children's favorite, Lincoln Logs, during their Christmas celebration on 967 Commercial Street in Weymouth. Thomas Kenney and Blanche Messier watch the children enjoy the gift during one of many holiday celebrations that the extended families shared.
Submitted by Dorothy Messier

SECOND GENERATION

Weiko Luoma started West Quincy Motors back in 1949. During a cold snap, he took this shot of wife Miriam and son Phil. Today, sons Phil and Doug keep the family business humming along.
Submitted by Doug Luoma

ICE AND SKY FLYER

Siblings (left to right) Michael, Mary and Joseph Iacobucci with friend Fred Gentile (second from left) spent many winter days with their faces pressed against the cold air skating at St. Moritz Pond. Joseph would later become an airplane mechanic for the U.S. Army. After the service, he owned and operated an automobile service station. Planes, however, remained a passion. Joseph refurbished and built planes throughout his life, flying recreationally out of Plymouth Airport and Cranland Airport in Hanson.
Submitted by Kathleen Kerr

SLIDE TO HOME

Joseph Cunniff, arriving home at 366 Hancock Street in Quincy after sledding, dutifully obeyed the "wear your hat" rule. His home was later moved to make way for the Sacred Heart School – where he would come to serve as Alumni Association president.
Submitted by Laurie Strout

SEASIDE VISIT

A visit to Plymouth Harbor has always been popular with South Shore residents. Friends Virginia Coletti and Josephine Vissa (left to right) pose in front of the replica of the Mayflower in 1957. Perhaps this seaside visit inspired wanderlust in Josephine, as she later left Quincy and moved to Paris.
Submitted by Ann Ramponi

LEAP FOR GIRLS

Who says girls are only about sugar and spice? Bonnie Babbitt, and sisters Jane and Ellen Ford of First Parish Road in Scituate caught pollywogs and frogs at the local pond and brought them home as pets.
Submitted by Ingrid Ford

WORKIN' ON MY TAN

Back in the 1930s, when a good day on the beach required white tan lines and not SPF 45, Lauretta (Butt) Cunniff (far right) shows off her spoils with sister Alice Butt (far left) at the Town River in Quincy.
Submitted by Laurie Strout

HAT'S OFF TO FRIENDSHIP

Before miniskirts and love beads, long-time chums Jean Marchetti Liben (left) and Sharon Mallar Donahue (right) of Quincy Point are suited and ready for Easter Sunday service at St. Joseph's Church in Quincy. Both women are graduates of Quincy High School and remain friends today—in spite of any bonnet envy that may have preoccupied their past!
Submitted by Jean Liben

CRAFT'S EXPRESS

Francis Courtney Sr. drove for Craft's Express of Milton, which was owned by Courtney's brother George. Craft's had two trucks garaged on Breck Street. In the 1940s, the men delivered meat and produce to businesses and estate homes in the area. One of their biggest customers was Bent's Cookie Factory, which supplied their water crackers to the U.S. Navy. *Submitted by Ellen Courtney*

IRISH IN QUINCY

Edward and Hannah Buckley emigrated from Ireland and the men of the family found work at the quarries. Pictured here in the late 19th century at their home on 36 Bates Avenue, their property abutted a quarry. Hannah took care of the linens for St. Mary's Church. *Submitted by Kathy Martinelli*

REAL GEMS

Benjamin Loring started Loring Jewelers in Plymouth in 1898 and it remained in the family for almost 100 years. Sons Bernhard and Charles "Lester" (left to right), with their associates, carried the business through the next generation. Many local couples sealed their vows with a Loring ring.
Submitted by Charles and Eileen Loring

NOT JUST A SNACK BUT A MEAL

Hassan's Variety on Southern Artery expanded their offerings to full meals and changed their name to Ma's Lunch to accommodate shipyard employees' growing demand for prepared food. Young Allie Hassan and older brother Samuel Hassan helped out.
Submitted by Zaida Shaw

BUSINESS PROWESS

Barbara (woman in picture) and Samuel Butt lived at 18 Ellerton Road in Quincy and had six children. Young Samuel "Buddy" (in carriage) was born in 1912, and became a prominent businessman after graduating from Bentley School of Accounting. He worked at the Fore River Shipyard and Firestone before becoming Vice President of Finance for A. Schulman Company of Ohio. Young Barbara (girl in picture) attended the Woodward School for Girls and Chandler Secretarial School in Boston. She worked at the Massachusetts Institute of Technology where she met her husband Edson DeCastro. DeCastro led the formation and development of Data General Corporation and for 22 years was its chief executive officer. *Submitted by Laurie Strout*

RIDING THE WHITE HORSE

From an early age, Detective Lieutenant Robert Perchard, liquor inspector for the City of Quincy Police Department, clearly was destined to come in riding the white horse. *Submitted by Linda Perchard*

FAMILY BUSINESS

Enterprising and ambitious, the Otis family operated a bakery, hair salon and tailor shop on
Gannet Road in North Scituate during the late 19th century.
Submitted by Richard Underhill

WEDDING PARTY

Shortly after their marriage, John and Lyda (LeVangie-Carol) Killory hosted a party at their home on Sachem Street in Wollaston – where they would live for the next 60 years and later raise three children. The couple met at United Fruit Co. where John was an accountant and Lyda was his secretary. Their professional relationship changed forever when one day John asked Lyda to come into his office and take this memo: "Lyda, will you go to Old Silver Beach with me on Saturday?"
Submitted by Elayne Quinn

MONSTER BASH

The Sorrentino house on Manzella Court was a lively destination during Halloween 1959. Left to right, monster Tommy Harris handles Margaret Stevens. Mike and Margaret Chapman get cozy. Sorrentino relatives frightful Jimmy, hillbilly Pat, and matriarch Frances Sorrentino. Amidst this scary bunch, is it any wonder that Frances is clutching her purse?
Submitted by Thomas Sorrentino

GRANDMA'S KITCHEN

Grandma's apple pie gets mixed up by tiny fingers. One-
and-a-half-year-old Marianne Maguire helps grandma
Lillian Mullin roll out the dough.
Submitted by Katharine Maguire

JUMP!

Happy and warm wearing the sweater her
mother made, Lillian Murphy keeps time
by rope, while friend Roberta Orenstein
plays hopscotch on the adjacent path.
Submitted by Lillian Murphy

DOTING GRANDPA

Arthur Maguire lived in California but loved to visit the kids and grandkids back East. On those visits, the Maguire girls would wait to hear grandpa's famous words, "Get your friends, we're going to Paragon Park." Kathleen Maguire, Susan Gavin, Marcia Gavin and Marianne Maguire all enjoy their cotton candy courtesy of Grandpa Arthur.
Submitted by Katherine Maguire

COASTER GIRL

Twelve-year-old Mary Flynn loved to ride Nantasket's Giant Coaster. The famous thrill-ride was built in 1917 and rebuilt in 1932 after a fire destroyed parts of the coaster. Pictured here in 1948, Mary might never have imagined that the colossal coaster would be moved to a Six Flags park in 1985, after Paragon Park's closing.
Submitted by Mary (Flynn) MacDonald

HOT FUN

Nantasket Beach has refreshed and amused more generations of South Shore residents than perhaps any other summer destination. Its life in the 1920s included the Hilarity Hall fun house, a dance pavilion hosting big band music, and the smell of salt-water taffy in the air. And it was as crowded then as it is today!

Submitted by Donald Griffin

MILLER'S MOTORS

In the early days of the automobile, the enterprising Lloyd Miller of Hull saw some unfilled market niches. Miller's Repair Shop serviced cars and boats, while his 1921 "One Ton" Ford Model TT provided emergency towing help to stranded South Shore motorists – like the gentleman pictured. For those without their own wheels, Mr. Miller operated Hull's first bus service.
Submitted by Bruce Simons

WOODEN BOAT

Fore River was not the only location for shipbuilding. Cliff Caseley, William Kitchen, Ronny Caseley and David Galbraith built this wooden boat for the Caseleys at home on Quincy Shore Drive and launched the vessel at Wollaston Beach. The baby, Norman Caseley, eventually inherited the craft, which has more than proven its seaworthiness.
Submitted by Jean Caseley

IRON SHARPENS IRON

The men of the FitzPatrick and Happenney Blacksmith shop – Lymon Burgin, Edward FitzPatrick, Pat Coakley, James Happenney and Mr. Gagnin (first name unknown). FitzPatrick and Happenney, apparently not scared of a little fire, also drive the West Corner Fire truck for the town.
Submitted by Kathleen Reichardt

SOLE MATES

John Heffernan and his son operated Heffernan's Shoe Store at 1359 Hancock Street in Quincy Square for nearly 70 years. This photo was taken in 1915.
From the Collection of Tom Galvin

POLITICAL HITS

U.S. Senators Mike Mansfield of Montana as umpire; John F. Kennedy of Massachusetts as catcher; and Scoop Jackson of Washington as batter, take their political hits during a fundraiser at the South Weymouth Naval Air Station during the early 1950s.
Submitted by Susan Jeffrey

RUNNING THE RACE

Senator John F. Kennedy and Mrs. Jacqueline Kennedy attend a political fundraiser at the South Weymouth Naval Air Base during his presidential run. The Kennedys are greeted by Albert Schofield, Lawrence Schofield, Mrs. Albert Schofield and Mrs. Lawrence Schofield.
Submitted by Susan Jeffrey

SCHOFIELD'S GARAGE

Sam H. Schofield was quite industrious. Schofield's Garage was part of a larger parcel of land he purchased in lower
Jackson Square, Weymouth, where he also built his home. The shop was decorated for a Fourth of July celebration
after World War I. Schofield's Garage was in business for approximately 90 years.
Submitted by Susan Jeffrey

AND THE BAND PLAYED ON

Jewelers Bernhard (bandleader/conductor) and Charles "Lester" Loring (second from right) earned extra money
during the Depression performing around the South Shore. The group became a popular local draw. Here, their
orchestra played for the 1928 New Year's Ball at the Plymouth Armory.

Submitted by Charles and Eileen Loring

AMAZING CATCH

Captain Eddie Fairweather aboard the "Barbara and Phyllis" caught a 1,200 lb. Great White off Plymouth during the winter of 1938. Market price for such a catch? A penny a pound.
Submitted by Skip DeBrusk

GROUNDING OF ETRUSCO

A most unusual sight for townspeople is now the stuff of legends. The 1956 grounding of the Italian ship Etrusco at Lighthouse Point in Scituate was captured by Ingrid Ford. Scituate residents housed and fed the seamen until arrangements could be made for their rescue and return.
Submitted by Ingrid Ford

STREET FIGHT

Lymon Burgin and Edward FitzPatrick do some recreational sparring outside the blacksmith shop where the men worked. Lymon's brother was a notable dentist in Hull and Edward was a master farrier known for his skill at shoeing horses.
Submitted by Kathleen Reichardt

DOUBLE DUTY

Twin brothers and Marines, Anthony and Augustine Belmonte of Quincy prepare to leave home and join their comrades for active duty in Japan.
Submitted by Maryliz Belmonte

WORK HORSE

Charles Anderson (bottom row, first from left) was a paid fireman for the Quincy Fire Department, seen here with his volunteer colleagues. His able horse made many heroic rides. Being so fond of the horse, Charles kept his tail after the animal's death.

Submitted by Paul Anderson

DRAKE HOMESTEAD

The namesake of Pembroke's Lydia Drake Library is seen, in 1888, with her bicycle at the Drake homestead.
Augustus Drake, her husband, manufactured shoes in the "Pine Room" of the home.
Submitted by the Lydia Drake Library

FOR WHOM THE BELLS TOLL

The Toll House Inn in Whitman, famous for the Toll House Cookie, was the setting for the marriage of Ruth Powers and Navyman John B. McDonald. This was one of the many "white" weddings of the early 1940s, with men in Naval uniforms and the bridal party dressed to match. This bride was the proprietress of the Ruth Powers School of Dancing in Weymouth.
Submitted by Dorothy Meisser

A MOTHER'S LOVE

For Lucy Smith, being the wife of a sea captain (Captain John Smith) meant that she spent much of her time attending to the children, without the day-to-day companionship of her spouse. But her days were active and filled caring for their many children. When Captain Smith returned from the sea, it was said that soon after, another child followed.
Submitted by Gertrude Tower Smith Bongarzone

DEVOTION

Granddaughter Carol Archer loved spending time with her grandparents on Hough's Neck. Young Carol was very proud of the flowers she had just picked for Grandma Theresa Holmes. Grandpa Holmes frequently went out fishing on his boat.
Submitted by Carol Archer

SHOWING SUPPORT
The 1958 Scituate High School
Cheerleading Squad
Submitted by Pat Galligan (second row on left)

TIME TO MAKE THE DONUTS

In 1950, the Open Kettle doughnut shop on Southern Artery changed its name to Dunkin' Donuts…and the rest is history!

From The Patriot Ledger Archives

STUNT MAN

Sven Becklin was quite a character. When he wasn't tossing wife Matlilda and daughter Elsa around in his wheelbarrow, he might have been pole vaulting over the family grape arbor or walking on his stilts. Sven was an avid cross-country skier and athlete in his native Sweden and made his living here in Weymouth as a carpenter. His granddaughter currently lives in the house he built on King Street where this photo was taken in 1919.
Submitted by Marcia Marland

WISH LIST

Sisters Carol, Judy and Elaine Lukkanen (left to right) of Quincy gleefully take their Christmas (1952) list right to the source. No sign of tears or fears on these faces – the sisters (all accomplished, married and still smiling) get together each Saturday to take their dad to lunch.
Submitted by John Lukkanen

THE SATUIT MARINE FLOAT

More economical and buoyant than timber counterparts, Mr. Fred S. Gilley's (second from right) 1956 invention – the Satuit Marine Float – was made from Styrofoam and sold throughout the East Coast. A 20 by 30 ft. float with an 8,000 lb. capacity sold for $1,850 precut.
Submitted by Beverly Westerveld

SERVICE—OUR MIDDLE NAME!

The United Service Organization (USO) of Quincy ran nightly programs from its inception on June 1, 1942 to its close on August 31, 1946. Religious and civic organizations and hundreds of local volunteers, like Dorothy Kelly of Quincy, hosted and provided entertainment for servicemen and defense personnel operating in the area.
Submitted by Dorothy Kelly

DADDY'S INDULGENCE

Arthur Earle Bennett's father spent much of his time away at sea. So when he returned to their Milton home, it was his pleasure to spoil the children with elaborate gifts. This fire engine, given to young Arthur around 1922, may have topped the list!
Submitted by James Bennette

HOLY SMOKE

Cousins Lillian Murphy and Frederick Joy received their First Communion at Sacred Heart Church in Quincy. But earlier that day, the children had some confessing to do. Just before taking this picture, the dressed-up pair was caught smoking their first cigarette in the garage! It must have been a pretty unpleasant experience all together because neither one ever smoked again!
Submitted by Lillian Murphy

YOUNG DISCIPLES

The Sunday School at St. Andrew's Episcopal Church in Hanover, circa 1935. Rev. Stanley Ross Fischer is on the left.

Submitted by Jean Migre

UNLIKELY BUSINESS OPPORTUNITY

Nothing like a sandwich or milk shake to liven up a day viewing a shipwreck! When the freighter Etrusco was grounded in Scituate Harbor, spectators arrived from miles around. Bill's Lunch Box moved in to provide refreshments and make a handy profit. Edith Becker with children Dave and Christine (foreground left) take in the sight. *Submitted by Dave Becker*

SEA LIFE
Skip DeBrusk, Captain Frank Savery, Rolly Bedard and Eddie Fairweather (left to right) steering cables and working the net out on Cape Cod Bay off Plymouth.
Submitted by Skip DeBrusk

TWO FISTED EATER

James E. Bennette (right) enjoys an ice cream, or two,
at a Wollaston Beach concession.
Submitted by Jim Bennette

LEWIS PAPER STORE

Sheldon Lewis ran Lewis Paper at 49 Beal Street from 1935 to
1960. The business offered cards, gifts and office supplies to retail
customers and paper and packaging supplies to wholesale clients.
Helen, his wife, worked by his side, typically six days a week,
serving customers and often doing the bookkeeping.
Submitted by Claire Currier

Submitted by Kathy Kerr

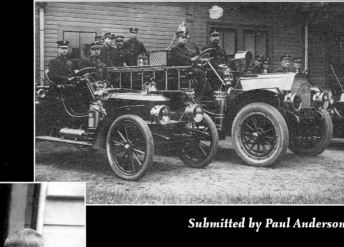

Submitted by Paul Anderson

Submitted by Carol Samuelian

Submitted by Shirley Back

Submitted by Richard Pompeo

Submitted by Ann Ramponi

Submitted by Joseph Walsh

Submitted by
Robin Ravida

Submitted by Marjorie Sullivan

Submitted by Gayle Sheehan

PONY EXPRESS

Young Charles A. Reardon of Merrymount and "Chubby," give the neighborhood kids a thrilling ride during the early 1930s.
Submitted by Charles A. Reardon

FUTURE OLD MAIDS?

The 1959 wedding of Tom Geraghty and Peg Cassidy shattered the validity of the moniker of Peg's informal college club, "Future Old Maids of America." Club members and friends of the bride include (left to right) Betty Franz, Dottie Galvin, Josephine Barra, Ruth Kelly, Jean Lynch, Marion Flaherty, Mary Callahan and Marie Nicholson. The reception was held at Dreamwold in Scituate.
Submitted by Ruth Kelly

MUSIC COMPANY

Drum roll, please, for the Boston Gear Works Band! Formed as a means of entertainment for the performers and listeners alike, Boston Gear Works provided many opportunities for employee involvement and recreation.
Submitted by John Croto, Boston Gear

RUB A DUB DUB

Baby Gwen (Roberts) Senger, here in 1930, enjoys a good soak in her back yard on Ocean Street in Quincy.
Submitted by Gwen Senger

RIVETING WORK
A riveting gang at the Fore River
Shipyard works on deck plates in 1919.
From the Collection of Tom Galvin

HIGH MINDED
Stunt dives off Fallon's Quarry was a key source of
entertainment for those diving...and those watching!
Submitted by Louis Malvesti

MEN OF STONE

Long days and sore limbs were the plight of the quarryman of Quincy – workers who truly earned their keep by the sweat of their brow. The quarry industry in Quincy began in earnest in 1825 and the Granite Railway, a civil engineering landmark, was established the next year. During the next 140 years, over 50 quarries would operate in Quincy.

Submitted by Gary Smith

HANCOCK AT HUNT STREET IN 1950

Before the "power lunch" was the Power Car Wash in North Quincy...also known as "wash mobile." Both it and the "flying A" logo of the Tydol Gas Station are but memories of an earlier Quincy.

From the Collection of Tom Galvin

WAY TOO FUN!

At the Weymouth Drive-In on Route 3A, pony rides were a featured attraction before the movie ever started! Young Chuck Hamilton's family would drive down from their home in Roxbury to take part in the fun.

Submitted by Judith Hamilton

STUFFED AND ROASTED FOR $1.95

The Greenview Farm in Weymouth on the Braintree line was known for
its farm-raised poultry and eggs. Their dressed and ready-to-eat chickens
and turkeys were a favorite on the way to or from Cape Cod.
From the Collection of Tom Galvin

HIT THE SLOPES
Ruth and George Kelly of Country Way in Scituate
pack up for a skiing and skating weekend away.
Submitted by Ruth Kelly

IRENE, MARGUERITE AND NANCY

The February 1927 shipwreck of the schooner *Nancy* off Nantasket Beach was a tourist attraction for many years until its hull finally was burned. But the real draw for the LeVangie sisters, Irene and Marguerite, are the surf and sand that has drawn generations to Nantasket's shore.
Submitted by Marguerite Footit

BEACH BABY

Once the cool salt water washes over tender toes, a kid gets hooked! Marianne Maguire gets help navigating the waves at Duxbury Beach with mom and dad, Katherine and Bob. Cookouts at the beach often followed their day in the surf.
Submitted by Katharine Maguire

BEFORE THE SEA WALL

Wollaston Beach from the bath house ramp – with views of the Wollaston and Squantum Yacht Clubs during the early 1920s.

From the Collection of Tom Galvin

RIDING HIGH

Brothers Eddie, Herb and Ray Skellett (standing), with friend, take a break from biking around the neighborhood (at Quincy Avenue and Faxon Park Road).
Submitted by Herbert Skellett

MEMORABLE SPOT

Bridesmaid Carol McCarthy and her mother Pauline Lacy at the 1958 wedding of Carol's high-school friend Alice Canniff at the Old Blacksmith Shop restaurant in Whitman.
Submitted by Carol McCarthy

"THE MOST YOU CAN SAVE IS THE LEAST YOU CAN DO"

A captured Japanese submarine and that tagline were rallying points used to encourage citizens to support the war effort and buy bonds. Joseph A. Messier archives the crowd's curiosity in front of the Thomas Crane Library in 1943.
Submitted by Dorothy Messier

CHRISTMAS PAGEANT

Sister Consillior's fourth grade class at the Sacred Heart School in Weymouth practiced long and hard to get to this moment! The pageant included holiday costumes from around the world, shepherds, angels and, of course, the Holy Family.
Submitted by Carol McCarthy

"E" FOR EXCELLENCE

In 1944, Wilfred B. Mathewson, president of Mathewson Machine Works accepts the Army-Navy E Award, an award pin issued to those who contributed to the national defense here at home. Quincy Mayor Thomas Burgin (third from left) observes.
Submitted by Wilfred Mathewson

YOUNG PATRIOT

In 1942, displaying national pride was particularly strong. Young Joey Messier, with cousin Mary Jane Kenney, shows off his new soldier's outfit. Joey also had a sailor uniform and an Uncle Sam costume.
Submitted by Dorothy Messier

STEEL-EYED

Joseph A. Messier was an electrical engineer for Bethlehem Steel with a keen, photographic eye. Mr. Messier was often called upon to chronicle ship launches and other major events. This photo shows the 1934 launch of the destroyer *USS Farragut* from the Fore River Shipyard. The ship served in the South Pacific during World War II and was moored at Pearl Harbor during the surprise attack by the Japanese in 1941.

Submitted by Dorothy Messier

BLACKSMITH SHOP

Edward FitzPatrick ran this blacksmith shop in Hingham's west corner during the 1940s on a site that was also a Gulf gas station.
Submitted by Kathleen Reichardt

KINGS AND QUEENS OF THE CASTLE

King's Castle amusement park of Whitman was a place of wonder and celebration for generations of South Shore children who remember climbing on the fire-breathing dragon, riding the Ferris wheel and eating sweet treats. The Becker children, David and Christine (second from left) with cousins Joanne (third from left) and Carolanne (first on left) squint and smile with Humpty Dumpty.
Submitted by Dave Becker

DUTY OF CARE

Marie Fehlow (second row, fourth from right) and her fellow 1946 graduates of the Quincy City Hospital School of Nursing are now ready to take on their duty of care. For Marie, that included service as an Army nurse – where she served in active and reserve duty for almost six years.
Submitted by Marie Fehlow

COURTING

John Trott and Margaret Davidson sparkle at Avalon Beach in 1929. John attended Thayer Academy and received a scholarship to Cornell. But he passed it over for a secure job at the shipyard and his sweetheart. The Trotts had three children and lived in Quincy.
Submitted by Robert Trott

HOT RHYTHMS

The Butcher Boy Drum Corps was the pride and soul of the Braintree Volunteer Fire Association. Named after the Butcher Boy apparatus, this late 19th century iteration of the band is seen near the Quincy Avenue Bridge over the Monatiquot River in East Braintree. Pictured standing (3rd from left) is a young Philip Sullivan – who later became a prominent attorney serving Quincy and Braintree. *Submitted by Marjorie Sullivan*

CHONITA

Woodward School students Viola Dubé, Sally MacCracken, Claire (Lewis) Currier, Harriet Goldstein, Virginia Ash, and Elinor Cooperstein on stage for the school's 1953 performance of the operetta *Chonita*. Claire Lewis Currier remains active in the school's alumni association and is its past president. *Submitted by Claire Currier*

KITCHEN KLATCH

The Anella Kitchen Band of Quincy blended the unique sounds of toasters, washboards, and kitchen utensils with drums, xylophone, banjo and accordion for a one-of-a-kind sound. Left to right, Gladys DeCelle, Dora Perry, Viola Frazier, Grace Frazier, Marion Campbell, Bart Hill, Val "Muggsy" Perry, and Director Ella Arnold were on the slate of performers at the 1939 World's Fair in New York.
Submitted by Lorrayne Paolucci

BALLERINA

Young Marilyn (LeBlanc) Masterson loved to dance and dreamed of becoming a ballerina. She studied and practiced for eight years at the Helen O'Brien Dance Studio in Quincy.
Submitted by Tom Masterson

GABALOTS

The "Gabalots" women's bowling team of Quincy had a championship year in 1935. The league provided a source of camaraderie and recreation for women during a time when such options were limited.
Submitted by Bob Corbin

WATER WEAR

Louise White, Catheryn Duane, James Duane, Mary Duane and Milly Fitts (left to right) are suited up for swimming at Avalon Beach in the early 1930s. John Duane, the father of the Duane's pictured, operated John J. Duane Wrecking Company, a prominent South Shore business.
Submitted by Joyce Oliver

ONCE, AND AGAIN

Marie (LaFayette) Whelpley got her money's worth out of her $8 prom dress from Filene's Basement. Seen here attending the 1955 Milton High School prom, with suitor, that season Marie and her dress also attended Boston College High School's prom, as well as Cathedral High School's.

Submitted by Marie (LaFayette) Whelpley

THE GATHERING

Hans and Teresa Homes (bottom left and third from left) immigrated from Sweden and Denmark, respectively. Many family gatherings were held at their son Harry's (top, center) home in Rockland. Daughter Dorothy (bottom, second from left) and her husband John Stewart (top, left) founded Stewart Candies, which supplied the Boston Garden with Big Daddy pops and other treats. The relationship gained young Carol (on lap) entrance into major Garden events where she met stars like The Lone Ranger and the Cisco Kid.

Submitted by Carol Archer

STOPPING TRAFFIC

Before automation, the Old Colony Railroad would employ "crossing attendants," to stop traffic prior to a train's crossing. During the nighttime, crossing attendants would swing a kerosene lantern to make their signal to cars. In preparation for oncoming trains, attendants would refer to the train schedules and wait for that whistle. Ida Banzi was stationed at Nelson Street in Plymouth.
Submitted Clare Montanari

TOM AND HUCK

Young adventurers Eddie Galligan and David Curran, as Tom and Huck – with "Shep," enjoy an end of summer 1948 picnic at Sandhills in Scituate.
Submitted by Patricia Galligan

THE OYSTER HOUSE

The Oyster House on 1657 Hancock Street served food and drink in a friendly atmosphere.
Mary (Hennebury) Adderly (first woman on left) was one such happy patron.
Submitted by Lorriane Daly

CAPTAIN OF HIS DOMAIN

Captain John Smith (left) of Cohasset was of Azorean descent. He was part owner of a 70-foot schooner, the E. A. Lombard, which traveled as far north as the Gulf of St. Lawrence and as far south as New Jersey in search of mackerel. His family is known for their connection to the old St. Anthony's Church in Cohasset (demolished in 1979), which he assisted in the building. His mother-in-law, Ignatia Concepcion Frates (center), in 1876, brought from the Azores a statue of the patron Saint—the church's first statue. Capt. Smith is pictured with his father-in-law, Captain Frates (second from left), wife Lucy (female adult on right) and children at his home in Cohasset.

Submitted by Gertrude Tower Smith Bongarzone

CONDUCTING BUSINESS

To support his family during the early 1900s, William H. Reardon (left) worked five days a week in a shoe factory and weekends as a conductor. Colleague George Higgins (right) and he are seen at the juncture of Route 53 and 123 in Hanover.

Submitted by Jean Migre

CHURCH PICNIC

The Scituate Baptist Church holds a Sunday school picnic in 1898.
Submitted by M.E. Von Iderstein

BABY COME HOME WITH ME

After her customary two-week hospital stay, a proud and rested Anna
Messier was escorted out of Quincy Hospital – homeward bound with
baby Joseph. Joseph distinguished himself by being the longest baby
of the bunch in the hospital nursery.
Submitted by Dorothy Messier

HIGH ASPIRATIONS

Born and raised in Quincy, it seemed natural that Harold Kavanaugh would spend his career working at the Fore River Shipyard – it was one of his favorite places to be. For many years, Harold was also President of the Fraternal Order of Eagles in Quincy.

Submitted by Barbara LaRosa

QUARRYMEN

John Coletti and foreman Roy Seavers pose in front of blocks of granite at the Hitchcock Quarry in Quincy. Granite extracted here was used in buildings all over the country, including at the South Shore National Bank at the corner of Maple and Hancock Street in Quincy.

Submitted by Ann Ramponi

ARNOLD SHOE

The Arnold Shoe Factory in Abington was where William H. Reardon (second from right) and fellow craftsmen spent their work week. Shoe factories were major employers and a significant economic driver for the South Shore.
Submitted by Jean Migre

A SHOE-IN FOR SUCCESS

Upon his arrival from England, Sam H. Schofield (right) went to work at the Carroll Shoe Factory in Weymouth in the early 1910s. It was hard, but profitable work and Schofield had his eye on greater success. He worked and saved and made investments into real estate, ultimately opening his own garage.

Submitted by Susan Jeffrey

CARROLL SHOE FACTORY

Pictured here in 1860, the Carroll Shoe factory was located in Weymouth.

Submitted by Susan Jeffrey

AUTO BIOGRAPHY

Buick Motors started in 1903 and South Shore Buick opened its doors in 1923. This 1927 used car sale at the dealership's then Hancock Street, Quincy location was meeting the demand for more affordable vehicles. South Shore Buick remains an important corporate citizen of the South Shore.

Submitted by Bob FitzGerald

BAKE ME A CAKE

These are the fine ladies who concocted those tasty cakes for Howard Johnson's – seen here across the street from the Elm Street, Quincy restaurant.
Submitted by Virginia Roccuzzo

BAKER MAN

Newcomb's Bakery was in business for 40 years before its closing in 1968. Daniel Newcomb learned the baking business while working at the A & P store. At one time, Newcomb's operated 13 shops in Greater Boston and points south. Dan Newcomb and daughter Louise (right to left), are seen here in 1930 at the Billings Road store in North Quincy. Son Richard, who continued the family tradition of food service, runs Newcomb's Farms Restaurants in Wollaston and Milton.
Submitted by Richard Newcomb

PEACH SUNDAES – 20 CENTS

Before the arrival of his roadside restaurants and hotels, Howard Johnson's first establishment sold toiletries, candies, cards, medicine – and that world-famous ice cream! Back in 1929, at his Beal Street store, HoJo's was selling a full quart of the frosty favorite for only 60 cents!

Submitted by Richard and Robin Pompeo

THE SPLENDID SPLINTER DRIVES IT HOME!

Pompeo Motors on Southern Artery sold cars to many Red Sox players who would pay cash and drive right off the lot. Alexander "Sam" Pomepo (fourth from left) is seen in 1949 with perhaps his most memorable customer, Ted Williams.
Submitted by Eleanor Anastos

BEECHWOOD POST OFFICE...AND VARIETY

E. Harold Brown was postmaster of the Beechwood (Cohasset) Post Office before it closed in the late 1950s. He also was the proprietor of a general store on the premises.
Submitted by Merle S. Brown

FILL IT UP

Service and smiles, from proprietor James J. Bearde
(center) and his friends (left to right) George Drew and
Michael Daven, at his Southern Artery Esso Station
for this 1954 snapshot.
Submitted by Brian Bearde

SWEET

Anna (DiSalvio) Durante was a cake maker
and decorator for the Howard Johnson's on
Elm Street in Quincy during the 1930s.
Submitted by Virginia Roccuzzo

ROLL BABY ROLL

Bethany Congregational Church's weekly pre-service "Cradle Roll" – this one held in the early 1900s – not only provided an opportunity to show off the little darlings in their Sunday best, but also was a meeting ground for Dorothy Fitts (baby in the large carriage on right) and Ralph Hayden (child sitting on his mother's lap). The two knew each other for nearly six decades before they married.

Submitted by Bethany Congregational Church

REFLECTIONS OF GERMANTOWN

Stan, John and Fred Marland lived in Germantown and played baseball in the open field in front of where their home was being built. The boys lived in a time when they rode a horse-drawn trolley to school. John became a candy maker and opened a candy store in Quincy, but moved to Weymouth as an adult as did his brother, Stan. Young Fred remained in Quincy.

Submitted by Marcia Marland

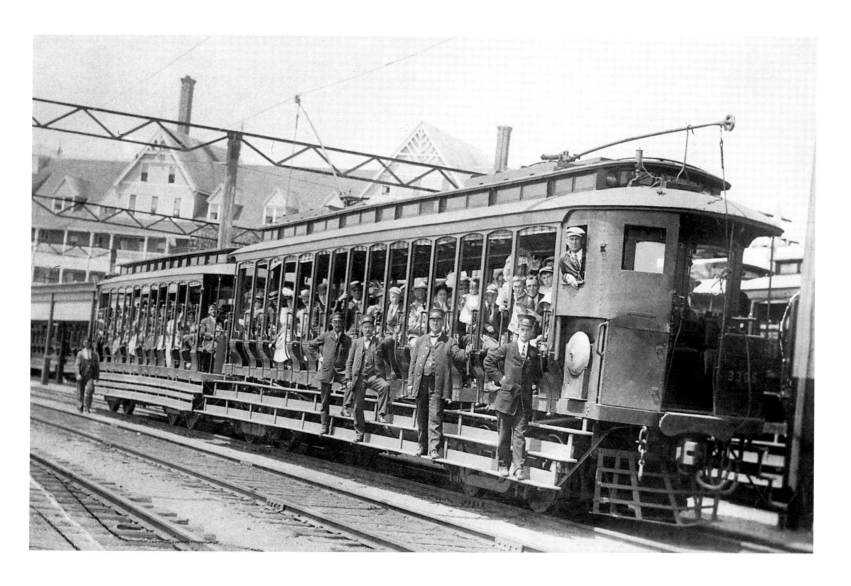

FINE LINE

Children, families and visitors on the Pemberton line, dressed in their finery, arrive at
Nantasket Beach via the Old Hull Trolley at the turn of the 19th century.

From The Patriot Ledger Archives

FRECKLES

The Buckley family of Milton were tremendous animal lovers, keeping horses, chickens and dogs. But Freckles, the family Irish Setter, was truly family. Tommy and Joan, posing here on Easter morning, just adored the canine. Long after his death, Joan kept a statue of her beloved pet on her mantle.
Submitted by Kathy Martinelli

BEACHING IT

Elinor Buckley's (front, right) grandmother's house on Walker Street in Quincy provided the perfect meeting place for her and her friends, all graduates of Milton High School, to gather for fun on Wollaston Beach. Elinor, described by her niece as "the most beautiful woman in the world," went on to graduate from the Katharine Gibbs School and have a career with the Social Security Administration office in Boston. Elinor loved to write poetry, and a special poem written for her father has become a family treasure.
Submitted by Kathy Martinelli

A LESSON IN FRIENDSHIP

Ellen "Nellie" Granahan and Josephine Kelly were Quincy schoolteachers from the late 1800s to the early 1930s. The longtime friends and traveling companions, here in retirement, relax in Nellie's garden at her Wollaston home.
Submitted by Kathy Martinelli

ONE GOOD CATCH

Dominick Brackett (right) lived in Dorchester and owned the Blue Point Tavern in Allston. He loved to come down to Hingham Harbor to clam and fish – this time showing his prize with great-grandson Tex Cusgrove at the Hingham town dock.
Submitted by Paul Healey

FOUNDATION OF FAITH

In September 1927, Bethany Congregational Church laid the foundation for its new Spear Street house of worship. It was the third building for this congregation – and remains its home today.

Submitted by Bethany Congregational Church

SUMMER FUN

Each year, a group of friends and neighbors on Little Sandy Pond in Weymouth would hold a traditional clambake, feasting on lobsters, corn and other local delicacies. Many Quincy residents had vacation cottages on Little Sandy Pond, including twin sisters Jean and Jane Adams and friend Peggy Heap, shown wearing bathing suits in the front row.

Submitted by Peggy Heap

SURE FOOTED

Miss Mildred Holmes' legendary dance and etiquette classes held at Christ Church Episcopal in Quincy accepted students city-wide. She taught the children the finer points of the craft, including how to make appropriate introductions to a dance partner and her parents. The $40 price tag per session proved valuable to dance class alum David Barton (back row, sixth from right), who was the only American GI in Germany who knew how to waltz!
Submitted by David Barton

BASEBALL BOYS

The Belmonte brothers Augustine (top row left), Anthony (second row left) and Paul (second row, third from left) nurtured their love for America's game by spending hours down at Kincaid Park in Quincy playing with the boys. Playing baseball at the park would be something the men would do for many more years to come.
Submitted by Maryliz Belmonte

ABOVE THE GLASS CEILING

Everyone knows that aviation pioneer Amelia Earhart broke numerous flying records. And many South Shore residents know that she was an incorporator of the Dennison Airport in Squantum. But Ms. Earhart has some other unique credits to her name. In 1928, she became aviation editor of Cosmopolitan magazine. Two years later, she helped organize a new airline, New York, Philadelphia and Washington Airways, and became its vice president of Public Relations.
From The Patriot Ledger Archives

BREAKING POINT

Quincy Point Garage proprietor Alexander "Sam" Pomper opened his shop in the early 1900s in a location
that could service the many autos which broke down on the road home from Nantasket Beach. It was a
shrewd idea that proved successful. The spare cash bought Sam an auto dealership just a half mile away.
Submitted by Eleanor Anastos

ROCKIN' L RANCH

George Litchfield's ranch off Webster Street in Hanover was the meeting ground for this group of friends who loved to ride and sing. Left to right George with crooner Frank Tedesco and strummer Al Tedesco in 1941. Frank still sings at local restaurants.
Submitted by Frank Tedesco

BOYS PLAY

The young brothers Skellett, (right to left) Eddie, Richie, Ray and Herb, with friend, loved to play kick the can, leapfrog and endless hours of baseball in the open area near their home on the corner of Quincy Avenue and Faxon Road in Quincy. Each of the brothers would later serve in the U.S. Navy. Herbert spent three years on destroyer ship *USS Niblack* between Casablanca, Sicily and southern France. His ship was credited with sinking the German submarine U-960 in May of 1944 in the Mediterranean and capturing its commander Günther Heinrich.
Submitted by Herbert Skellett

SHOPPERSTOWN

Hancock Street in Quincy was a popular destination for South Shore shoppers in the 1950s. Promoted as "Shopperstown," Quincy Center featured a number of well known retailers, including Fanny Farmer and Kresge, a five & dime store which later evolved into Kmart.

From The Patriot Ledger Archives

CRACKER LADIES

In 1801, Josiah Bent began baking biscuits in his Highland Street home in Milton, Massachusetts. One day, he over-baked his biscuits and a "crackling" sound emitted from the brick oven. Thus, he coined a new American phrase, "cracker," and began a tradition of cracker-making in Milton that continues today. The "Cracker Ladies" of Bent's in 1948, (left to right) Jennie Brown, Winnie Byrne, Florence Turner and Kitty Munche hand-pack the famous Cold Water crackers.
Submitted by James Pierotti, Bent's Cookie Factory

KING OF QUEENS

Under the shadow of Our Lady and many lovely ladies, young Dan Murphy helps usher in the May Procession at Holy Ghost Church in Whitman.
Submitted by Dan Murphy

FLOATING IDEAS

This float from the 1925 Quincy Tercentennial parade celebration
was an attractive way to influence opinion. The week-long
tercentennial event drew visitors from all over the region.
Submitted by Richard Pompeo

MAKING A DIFFERENCE

During the late 1920s the Hall children of Berry Street in Quincy were
busy just being kids. But as they grew, they – like their parents – became
active in community and spiritual life. Pryor Hall Jr. (left) became Grand
Knight of the Knights of Columbus and played baseball for the Quincy
Comets. Frankie Hall was a soloist at St. John's Church. Young Marion
Hall would eventually enter the Sisters of St. Joseph in Boston.
Submitted by Marion Hall

CAROL'S BREATH

The devastating force of Hurricane Carol in August 1954, facing Squantum, is powerfully preserved by Charles Flagg. Homes in Hull were destroyed, and much of the South Shore was without power. Cookouts became a popular scene in neighborhoods.
Submitted by Charles Flagg

CALM AFTER THE STORM

The Great New England Hurricane of 1938 was one of the most destructive and powerful storms ever to strike Southern New England. The Samuelians of Quincy weathered it all right, and young Carole looks positively gleeful perched on the downed tree in her yard at 46 Division Street. Carole went on to graduate from the Woodward School for Girls and Curry College before joining the family business – Seymours Ice Cream of Boston.
Submitted by Carole Samuelian

HOME ROW

In August of 1955, the region was struck with one-two punches by Hurricanes Connie and, a week later, Diane.
Some areas received up to 20 inches of water over a two-day period. Weymouth reeled in the aftermath.
Submitted by Dave Belcher

UNDER COVER

In 1942, a group of scientists covertly working in Jackson Square, East Weymouth were helping the war effort by building state-of-the-art microwave radar equipment designed by the Radiation Lab at MIT. The classified project was led by Ralph Tedesco (third from left), Al Tedesco (third from right) and Norman Loud (second from right). Norman was also head of the Science Department at Weymouth High School.
Submitted by Frank Tedesco

OVERBOARD IN LOVE

Shirley Johnson met John Back when he was working at the Fore River Shipyard. When John enlisted in the Navy, the pair continued to visit at the ports of Norfolk, VA and Newport, RI, where he was stationed. John took a three-day pass in May of 1943 to marry his girl. He returned from leave a married man, but on day four, was declared AWOL. John never minded, the latter designation was a joyful reminder of how much more he gained that weekend. John and Shirley Back recently celebrated their 60th wedding anniversary.
Submitted by Shirley Back

PROTECTING THE HOMELAND
United States Army Corporal Dave Becker was trained to defend the East Coast in the event of an attack at Camp Edwards in Cedarville using this water-cooled, 50-caliber machine gun.
Submitted by Dave Becker

PATRIOT FLYERS
With the threat of War looming, these South Shore men received pilot training in 1941 from the U.S. Navy at an auxiliary field at Squantum. The effort prepared George Haviland (second from left), Arthur Desmond (third from left), Ralph Tedesco (bottom left) and the other civilian patriots for combat.
Submitted by Frank Tedesco

Submitted by Jim Bennette

Submitted by Dorothy Kelley

Submitted by Zaida Shaw

Submitted by Paul Prusik

Submitted by Dan Sullivan

GENERATIONS

Bradford Hawes (center top) served as patriarch of a large and attractive family, most members of which lived in Weymouth. The extended family, gathered here for a ceremony honoring Miles Standish in 1923, included relatives with surnames of Gerstley and Mathewson.

Submitted by Donald Mathewson

GOOD SPORTS

William "Sonny" Miller of Marshfield (second from left), Anna Miller Pooler of Scituate (second from right) and Lillian Miller Willis (far right) of Hull sporting a fresh catch with a neighbor friend in front of their dad's shop (Miller's Boat Shop) at the Corner of Hull's U Street and Nantasket Avenue in 1940.
Submitted by Bruce Simons

FISHING AROUND

Pauline (Parker) Pyle summered with her family at Billington Sea in Plymouth and through those years became adept at getting her daily catch. Her skill at "fishing around" served her well as Duxbury correspondent and later a general assignment reporter for *The Patriot Ledger*, where she worked for nearly thirty years.
Submitted by Pauline Parker Pyle

BILLY GOATS THREE

The Courtney cousins of Capen Street in Milton enjoy their Billy goat ride on the homestead while the fathers, Francis and Michael Courtney, look on. Nearly 80 years later, a fifth generation of Courtneys resides next door.
Submitted by Ellen Courtney

SNOW TIME LIKE WINTER

Ten-year old Bernice Murphy's winter dreams have come true during the season of 1947-48, when snowfall was particularly high – making for some terrific sledding!
Submitted by Bernice Murphy

CHAMPS

Dad, Joseph Cunniff, coached a winning season during the mid-1950s for the Quincy Yankees
with sons Bill and Eddie (bottom row, second and third from left).
Submitted by Laurie Strout

ON LAND AND SEA

Marchers representing the Fore River Shipyard parade through Quincy as part of the city's tercentenary celebration in 1925.
The parade was so large that it was grouped into "divisions" that included military, civic, trades, industry and schools.
Submitted by Dorothy Stephenson

FORWARD MARCH

Cheering on the home team at Veteran's Stadium, the 50-member 1941 Quincy High School Band was accompanied by lovely and talented majorettes (left to right) Marjorie Corcannon, Shirley Johnson, Dora Tocia, head majorette Marjery Comis, Dotty Pedrette, Leona Bonome, and Lois Kintigh.
Submitted by Shirley (Johnson) Back

SMITTEN

In 1952, Michael Patrick King takes the hand of his new bride Rose Kippenberger King outside St. Mary's of the Hills Church in Milton – the same house of worship where their three children would later be christened and married. The young groom looks eager to move the reception along quickly!
Submitted by Joanne Brundage

AGROUND

The memorable 1956 grounding of the Italian freighter *Etrusco* at Lighthouse Point in Scituate is captured here in grand scale.

Submitted by Lorraine Quinn and Andrea Santoro

ADAMS ACADEMY

The Adams Academy was designed in 1869, opened in 1872, and operated as a boy's school until 1907. The first class had 23 students, six of whom were from Quincy. Among its early students were sons of the Adams family. The Academy was built under the supervision of John Quincy Adams' son, Charles Francis Adams, by leading Boston architects William Robert Ware and Henry Van Brunt. Ware was asked by the Massachusetts Institute of Technology to establish the first university-based school of architecture in the United States. The Academy building is now home of the Quincy Historical Society, which also oversees its maintenance.

Submitted by Brian Bearde

QUINCY NINE

Baseball was truly America's pastime in 1918, when this photo of the Quincy High School baseball team was taken. Coincidentally, it was also the last year the Boston Red Sox won the World Series. Edwin J. Heap, shown in the front row at left, went on to play college baseball at MIT.

Submitted by Peggy Heap

TEAM BUILDING

Clark & Smith construction company sponsored this trophy-winning baseball team in the 1950s with Louie DiNicola (top row, far right) and Anthony Belmonte (second row on the left). The men played at Kincaide Park in Quincy.

Submitted by Maryliz Belmonte

LIVE WIRE

Joseph Kippenberger, after loosening up a bit, decided he'd join the band at his sister Rose's wedding in Milton. We're not sure what the band thought of that. And we can only imagine what the nice young women to the right of him were thinking. Joe, an electrician by trade, was truly the live wire of the family. He sometimes wet his fingers and put them in a light socket just to see what would happen and get the attention of those watching!

Submitted by Joanne Brundage

SECOND ACT

Lyda (LeVangie) Carol (right) and her sister Eva (LeVangie) Connolly (left), known to Vaudeville audiences as the "Dolly Sisters," traded in their dancing shoes for wedding slippers and baby booties! Lyda's second act would prove just the beginning of her changing roles. Not long after her marriage to Albert Carol, he died of tuberculosis. She needed to support her family, but returning to her old career was not a viable option. Lyda learned to type, got a job, and became the most proficient typist in the pool! Now that's an award-winning performance!
Submitted by Maureen Boda

CLASS ACT

Sixth graders at the Vose School in 1949 in Milton dress it up. (Top, left to right) Jane Tufts, Jane McGrath, Carol Naughton, Natalie Lawler. (Top, right to left) Dorothy Fashay, Marita Manning. (Bottom left to right) Lawrence Forte, Kendall Richards, Howard Grossman, Marlene Thurston, Regina Match, Tom Masterson.
Submitted by Tom Masterson

Celebrating 100 years of providing health care with compassion, dignity and respect.

Since 1903, Milton Hospital has made a commitment to improving the health of the community by providing quality, personalized health care with compassion, dignity and respect. The roots of this tradition began in a small convalescent home in Milton near the turn of the century. By 1903, the institution had become Milton Hospital. Over time, Milton Hospital has evolved to meet the needs of the community.

Milton Hospital has more than 300 physicians on staff who provide a complete complement of inpatient and outpatient services including comprehensive diagnostic care, 24-hour emergency services, ambulatory care and transitional care. As we enter our second century of caring, we look forward to bringing our patients our unique brand of caring and compassionate medicine.

Milton Hospital

92 Highland Street
Milton, MA 02186
617-696-4600

126

Hassan Brothers Jeep - Serving the South Shore since 1946

Established in 1946, this landmark Quincy business was founded by four brothers, Fauthal, Joseph, Mustafa and Abdo "Turk" Hassan. Beginning as a Nash dealership, the business moved to its present location on Washington Street in 1953. In 1977, Hassan Brothers became a Jeep dealership that continues to sell and service the legendary American-made Jeep vehicles. Still family owned and operated, the dealership is now run by a second generation of Hassan brothers, John, David and Donald who proudly carry on the tradition of superior sales and service begun by "Turk" Hassan and his brothers.

HASSAN BROS. JEEP
617-773-8810

Quirk Auto Dealerships and the Fore River Shipyard
Leaders in Transportation

A Proud Tradition Continues...

Since its beginnings in 1901, The Fore River Shipyard has sent to sea an incredible array of ships and had a lasting impact on American history. Many of the ships built here were instrumental in helping America win World War I and World War II. Now this historic site will be used by a South Shore business that also plays an important role in the transportation industry.

In 1977, Daniel Quirk purchased his first auto dealership in Massachusetts. Since that time Quirk Automotive has grown to be one of the largest volume auto dealers in the Boston area – with over 600 full and part-time employees. The purchase of the Fore River shipyard by Quirk Automotive will help this historic site continue to play a prominent role in the transportation industry.

QUIRK AUTO DEALERSHIPS
FORE RIVER SHIPYARD
BRAINTREE • QUINCY

A Continuing Tradition of Excellence in Business

The **South Shore Chamber of Commerce** began in 1901, when Quincy's business leaders, led by Charles Francis Adams, chartered the Quincy Board of Trade. Over the years, the organization changed its name – to the Quincy Chamber of Commerce, the Quincy-South Shore Chamber, and then to the **South Shore Chamber of Commerce**. It has grown and evolved as the area's economy has grown and evolved.

Today, this non-profit organization is the largest chamber of commerce in eastern Massachusetts, representing more than 2,200 companies from sole proprietorships to multi-national, multi-billion dollar companies. Completely governed by its members, the **South Shore Chamber of Commerce** continues its tradition of helping local businesses by providing opportunities to build their network of business contacts, offering workshops and seminars to help them run their companies more effectively, pooling their buying power to access better employee benefits, meeting with top government and business leaders, and promoting their products and services.

On Beacon Hill, in Washington, and in city and town halls throughout the area, the **South Shore Chamber** is recognized as an effective voice for business and for the economic well being of the region.

John Blake, chairman of the 1965 annual chamber dinner meeting, presents a caricature to Howard B. Johnson. From left are: Mayor Amelio Della Chiesa, Blake Johnson, William J. Martin Jr. and Dr. Bradford E. Gale.

South Shore Chamber of Commerce
The Chamber and you...

617-479-1111
www.southshorechamber.org

129

New England Appliance and more, Inc.
Three Generations in the Appliance Business

This family business was started in 1936 by Larry Newcomb's grandfather, Phillip Pingree. Located on Commercial Street in East Weymouth, the shop was well known throughout the South Shore for selling and repairing radios, TV's, washer and dryers, refrigerators and other items. Larry's father, Wally Newcomb, took the business over in the 1950's.

Larry Newcomb first started working in the family business as a young boy, learning how to repair appliances. Eventually, Larry took the business over and expanded it to offer even greater value and service. Larry's hard work and determination paid off and the business has been rated #1 in the magazine Never Pay Retail and was also featured on the television show Chronicle. Today, as a third generation family business New England Appliance is proud to offer unbeatable deals on new appliances plus one of the largest "scratch and dent" departments in the country for those seeking even greater bargains.

Wesley Pingree, Phillip Pingree and an employee of the store with a radio designed by Phillip in the 1930's.

New England Appliance
and more, Inc.

236 Wood Road • Braintree • 781-848-3933

WEYMOUTH BANK
A special dedication to the community

In 1877, the Massachusetts Legislature enacted legislation enabling communities to form cooperative banks for the express purpose of promoting home ownership. Twelve years later in Weymouth, some prominent citizens chartered the South Weymouth Cooperative Bank - the town's first cooperative bank. In 1981, North and South Weymouth Cooperative Banks joined to become **Weymouth Bank**. From its humble beginnings, **Weymouth Bank** has evolved into a full-service community bank offering a broad array of products and services.

Much has changed over the past one hundred years, but our commitment to serving the community is as strong as ever. As an independent community bank, we will continue to serve Weymouth, Kingston and the South Shore by offering high-quality products and superior customer service. **Weymouth Bank** is committed to remaining an active supporter of our local community through our support of youth sports, local charities, and public projects.

WEYMOUTH BANK
S. Weymouth
E. Weymouth
Kingston
781-337-8000

www.weymouthbank.com

Member FDIC   Member SIF

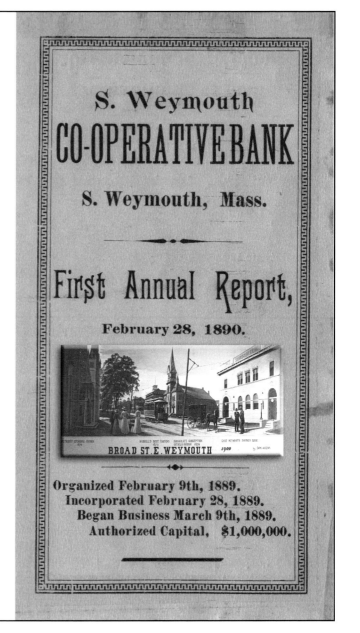

S. Weymouth
CO-OPERATIVE BANK
S. Weymouth, Mass.

First Annual Report,
February 28, 1890.

BROAD ST. E. WEYMOUTH   1900

Organized February 9th, 1889.
Incorporated February 28, 1889.
Began Business March 9th, 1889.
Authorized Capital, $1,000,000.

131

Jack Conway, Founder

THE SOUTH SHORE

Jack **Conway**, REALTOR®

is Conway Country

1974

(l. to r.) Patti Conway, Dick Cahill, Mayor Walter Hannon, Rita Sweeney,
Carol Conway and Jack Conway open Quincy sales office Oct. 17, 1974.

A Message from Jack Conway, Chairman, Jack Conway & Co., Realtor

It has been lots of fun over 46 years. We've built a one-man business, which started in Hingham Square, into the largest privately owned real estate company in Massachusetts and Northern New England.

Our 41 Southeastern Massachusetts sales offices and 750 people work as a team to make this continue to happen. The goal is to make sure our customers are happy and satisfied. If that happens, we all win — the buyers, the sellers, and we win, too.

We have been involved in tens of thousands of real estate transactions and have done many billions of dollars in sales but we, hopefully, have not lost our personal touch with the communities that we serve.

We've played leadership roles at the Chambers of Commerce, at the South Shore and Quincy Hospitals, at local and national real estate boards.

Success in this type of business is all about involvement and participation in community and civic affairs. It's about knowing and helping our customers.

Our plans for the future hinge on a work ethic of playing the game on the level and making sure that the customer comes out a winner. We appreciate your business and your friendship.

Jack Conway

www.jackconway.com

1961

Jack Conway records his first WBZ radio
ad with Dave Maynard Sept. 10, 1961.

Jack Conway & Co., REALTOR®
Your Neighborhood Realtor Since 1957
H.Q. 137 Washington St., Norwell (781) 871-0080 / Quincy Office 253 Beale St. (617) 479-1500